i

Emotions
A Book of Poem Stories

Fannie M. Hudson

New Smyrna

iii

First Paperback Edition 2015
Printed in the United States of America

ISBN-13: 978-0-9792196-3-4
ISBN-10: 0-9792196-3-9

Edited by
Janis F. Kearney
Published by
Fannie Minson Hudson

Email: pnm@parishnurseministries.org

Dedication

I dedicate this writing to God the Father, Son, Holy Spirit, and James, my best friend and husband.

James, you have always been my strongest supporters even when I had no idea you were. Thank you for the strength and encouragement that you give so unselfishly.

I thank God every day for giving me you James. And, James I thank you for hanging in there with me.

FOREWORD
Former President William J. Clinton's Diarist, Janis F. Kearney

Poetry is a baring of our soul and our spirit – our deepest, most protected of emotions. It is a difficult feat for any writer. We seldom are as honest with ourselves as we think we are, and even less often do we share our deepest truths with others. When we do, it is a very special moment – one human expressing a part of themselves that only God knows better than we, ourselves. This is a moment of awesomeness because, for that magical moment, we engender all that is good in the human spirit.

As a writer of prose, I have always held poets in the highest esteem. I am amazed that poets refuse to hide between the fluff and unnecessary verbiage of prose writers. They don't dance around the facts or issues. They don't take all day to say what can be said in one second, or at least one minute. They give it to you straight. Writing poetry is the writer at his or her most powerful... a moment of unparalleled vulnerability.

Fannie Hudson has offered up a portion of her soul, her spirit, her deepest *Emotions*, in this book of poetry. She has scraped the depths and ascended to the heights of our loves, hates, hurts, and confusion. Her poetry leaves no stone unturned. It touches on the love of parenting, the pain of romantic love; the infinity of friendships, and the destructiveness of jealous hearts.

I dare you, reader, to walk away from this book with your soul, your spirit still folded neatly within you.

You will be touched. You will be challenged. You will travel, poem after poem, through a troubling, but wonderful journey of *Emotions*.

Janis F. Kearney

Table of Contents

Introduction

Emotions, good, bad, happy, sad, or indifferent; are all part of us. What we do with our emotions have a lot to do with how we look at things in our life, and our world.

Positive emotions can carry us a long way. Positive emotions help us cope with the good times, and help us deal with the not so good times. Most import of all, we must be present to have them.

Take fear, we would rather not have it, sometimes it is hard to control it.

Love, we all want it, but don't always receive it, nor give it.

Faith, is there for each of us, free, we just have to believe, in order to receive it.

Misunderstanding is one emotion, that nobody wants, needs, likes, or understand.

However, we let our emotions control us, and sometimes get ahead of common sense.

How? Our imagination and insecurities embrace our fears, letting our thoughts and instinct for survival (or is it selfishness), cloud our judgment.

We may not find the answer for every reason, reaction, cause, or cure for our emotional moments. We can try to understand how others feel, and help them have a better day, by keeping our hurtful words at bay.

Love

Love is for beings,
and not things.

Love is felt,
shown,
and seen.

Love is a gift,
not bought or sold.

Love gives life meaning,
try it and see.

Without love, many things,
could never be.

Wisdom

Wisdom is precious,
though rare.

With wisdom you will learn,
know, and become aware.

To have wisdom is a definite plus.

Wisdom like love,
for a happy life is a must.

Alone

Alone by choice brings,
comfort and trust.

Alone by force,
is cruel and unjust.

Secrets

Secrets are good,
if they bring us joy and trust.

Secrets are bad,
if they bring hurt and destruction to us.

My Mommy

I had the best mommy in the world,
she use to call me "her girl".

Mommy would give me the biggest hugs,
making me feel all safe and snug.

My mommy saved special times,
just for her and me,
and special, that time would be.

My mommy made me feel special too,
giving me love and confidence,
encouraging me to use common sense,
saying "choose well my love,
don't be the kind to sit on the fence".

I can still feel her sweetness in the air,
her being gone still don't seem fair.

Mommy I love you and miss you so,
losing you was such a blow.

Fear

Fear is often misunderstood.

Is it respect and admiration beyond words?

Or is fear misplaced caution and dread?

Or is fear waiting for uncertainly,
and the imagination to be fed?

Fear can cause you to hate,
being unkind to friends and mates.

Don't let fear win,
reacting to fear can cause sin.

Hate

Have a taste of eternity.

Lean to love your enemy.

To know is to understand.

Don't try conquering one another.

Because after all,
you are my brother.

Father

Leader and friend.

Protector above all men.

Feared, respected, and revered.

Giver of love,
kindness, wisdom, and cheers.

Your honor is beyond compare.

A man like you,
found nowhere.

Understanding

Understanding is the gate between,
ignorance, knowledge, and wisdom.

Learn them, and their difference,
and achieve greatness.

Good and Evil

Good and Evil are not equal,
nor can they ever be.

God made both,
for a reason.

Trust Him and see.

Truth and Lies

Can hurt or heal.

Give life or kill.

Build courage or destroy.

Bring sorrow or joy.

Make you love or hate.

Will you have time to decide,
before it is too late?

Confusion

Confusion's author is clear.

Confusion like lies will cause incidents.

For confusion to work,
you must consent,
and be a part of it.

Honor

Honor does not live in strife.

Honor does not demand one's life.

Honor like valor will go before us.

Honor is bold and won't deceive us.

Honor is sure and strong.

Honor will not leave us,
lonely, or alone.

Somethings To Think About

Love

Hate

Hope

God

Trust

Joy

Discipline

Jesus Christ

Sacrifice

Admiration

The Holy Ghost
Faith

Judgment Day

Eternity

You

What People Share

Kind and well-meaning people,
encourage and cheer.

Hateful and ill meaning people,
discourage and sneer.

If there is sadness or pain,
kind people bring kindness,
because hope and helpfulness,
is their ultimate aim.

Pain

Pain can hurt,
to the depths of one's soul.

As long as there is pain,
one is alive.

Do something about it,
yell, scream, cry, sigh.

Worry

Worry will not change a thing,
worry will not give us wings,
or make us feel like kings.

If anything, worry, will make us sad,
and often make us feel bad.

All for nothing some might say,
all that worrying just made us pray.

Worry, worry not,
let us be thankful for what we got.

Trust in the Lord with all your heart, and lean not on
your own understanding; in all your ways acknowledge
Him, and He shall direct your paths. (Proverbs 3:5-6)

Thank you

Thank you for all that you have done yes,
we know you could have given some,
all or none.

You cared enough to give us all you had
for this kind gesture,
we are truly glad.

Thanking you can never be enough
you stand by us
even when things and times get tough.

Why?

Because your love goes beyond words or thoughts you
said we could do the same,
if we are willing to love, learn,
and be taught.

Easy

Loving you is easy,
you give so much in return,
with open arms to you we run,

Loving you is like,
a breath of fresh air.

Without you,
our lives would be in despair.

You came to show us the way,
and we know,
you will return for us one day.

We Can Too

Yes,
we can be like you,
in everything we do.

Some said it can't be done,
from those people we should run.

Just who do you believe,
them,
of course not,
with you at our side,
nothing is impossible,
for us to attain, gain, or achieve.

Everything

Means all we have,
everything, like a healing salve.

Holding nothing back,
can and will,
keep us on track.

Half of nothing is not enough.

After all none of it
is really our stuff.

To Him it all belongs.

Everything is what He gave,
and now,
do we think it's time to save?

Hold nothing back,
stay on track.

Grace

Grace is a beautiful word,
for all,
mankind, animal, fish, or bird.

Grace comes accompanied by mercy,
to show us the way,
to help us find Jesus,
and Heaven,
on that Glorious Day.

Will we be ready?

Something To Say

Are you Happy?

Did you have something to Eat?

Did you thank God this morning,
for letting you land on your feet?

Silence?

Is it because you have done me wrong,
for so long,
and I love you anyway?

Are you just silent,
and really have nothing to say?

Wisdom's Wise Domain-1

To seek wisdom from God,
is the first step
toward God's wise domain.

To love God,
is the second step
toward God's wiser domain.

To love one another,
is the third step
toward God's wisest domain.

The ability to love is a simple act,
that comes from with-in.

No one had to prepare us
to give or accept love.

Love just is,
a gift to us,
from God's Wise Domain.

Wisdom's Wise Domain-2

Wisdom asks for nothing in return.

It help bosses manage wisely.

It helps mothers nurture wisely.

It helps fathers protect
provide and respect,
his family wisely.

It helps children obey their parents timely.

It helps Christians treat others with respect,
always,
continuously and wisely.

There is no reason for being
unkind and unwise,
they just happen to go together.

Is there a remedy for them?

Yes, it is Wisdom's Wise Domain.

Wisdom's Wise Domain-3

Love is
God's Wisdom,
Good and Wise.

Let love and wisdom be your guides,
in all that you say and do,
and that same love and wisdom,
will come back to you.

Happy Valentine's Day
From God the Father,
Jesus the Son,
and the Holy Ghost.

God's Wisdom and Wise Domain.

My Real Friend

I told you the truth,
I am your real friend.

I love you
more than life,
and health.

By dying for you,
I gave of myself.

All I ask from you in return,
is be true to me,
and everyone I love.

Open Your Eyes

Open your eyes so you can see,
closing them
won't make your enemies flee.

Amazing Grace is not just a song,
if you use wisdom plus faith,
and you are strong,
you can fight evil all day long.

If you listen hard to what's being said,
your spiritual eyes will open,
and you can look ahead.

Mother and Friend

At church my friend learned
her mother had passed away.

First shock, confusion, and pain.

Feeling helpless, alone, and afraid.

With her pain I felt my loss,
of so many years ago.

I ask my friend to talk about
her mother's life.

She did so immediately,
with looks of love and peace in her eyes,
giving us both comfort and relief.

You see,
my friend and her mother were friends,
just as my mother and I had been.

Home-less and Chrome-less

What did I do?

I burned my bridges,
emptied my moats,
and cut down my ridges.

Oh, what a fool.

I would not listen,
or follow the rules.

You called me selfish,
and I called you cruel.

So, now I am home-less and chrome-less.
Now I know what do.

Learn to take care of me,
and my belongings too.

Heartbreaking Dreams-1

Last night in a dream,
I saw the other woman,
I wondered what did it all mean.

I saw you kiss her,
I saw you holding her hand,
all I could do was cry,
because I didn't understand.

I sacrificed all that I had,
I even delayed carrying out my plans.

Last night in a dream,
you tried holding on to me,
I love you still,
but my dream sets me free.

Heartbreaking Dreams-2

So today when I walked into that place,
and saw you looking into her face,
my dream was real,
and I know how other women must feel.

My heart was heavy,
it hurt my chest really bad.

Since I know what happened to me,
I am no longer sad,
only glad.

That heartbreaking dream
gave me the love of God,
peace of mind and strength I need,
to be on my own team.

Goodbye.

Small Beginnings

From small beginnings we came.

To give,
to share,
and be humane.

To love,
explore and adore,

To make peace,
and cause hate to cease.

From small beginnings,
to larger winnings.

One small step at a time,
will help us make,
the largest climb.

Innocence

Fresh like the smell of a baby's breath.

No if's, and, or maybe's, the sight of a baby,
will open your heart,
to God's work of art.

Soft like the touch of a baby's skin,
innocence is one or the other,
love, friend, foe, or kin.

Eyes open wide and trusting,
nothing cruel, distasteful, or disgusting.

Innocence's causes are pure,
no deceit, revenge, or backbiting,
but kindness, loving, and sure.

Your Mighty Arms

Your mighty arms,
they embrace me in times of laughter.

They make me feel safe,
and keep me from all harm,
today and forever after.

You look into my heart,
and know my inner workings,
and help me to endure.

Your mighty arms help my love,
stay in the right place,
and teaches me about your loving grace.

Your love is secure
your mercy is steadfast,
and shall withstand the passing of time.

In your mighty arms,
those you love, and love you in return,
are protected from all harm.

Abusive Love

You hit me, then say you are sorry.

You hurt me, then say don't worry.

I have to hide my fears,
many times I have no tears.

Do others have the same problem,
I wonder?

When our friends come around,
he acts good in front of them,
but when they leave,
the devil gets back into him.

Our friends laugh,
they don't know,
the pressure I'm under.

Why don't I leave, but to him I cleave.

We've been taught,
it wasn't done,
unless he gets caught.

I'm telling you be alert,
because love does not hurt.

Truth

Can set you free
or
Will make you flee.

Will make you hide
or
Will open you eyes.

Truth or dare is just the devil's snare.

Making you pretend you don't really care.

Real truth will set you free.

Good news, or bad news,
the truth will always be.

Freedom

Freedom has always been Free,
God has always said come and follow me.

Such as I have I will give thee,
willingness of heart
and obedience is the key.

Father, Holy Spirit, and He,
Jesus died so we could stay free.

Give God and Jesus a try,
tell sin and hatred goodbye,
and have eternal life.

All About Jesus

It is all about You, Jesus.

Some people often wonder,
why you came at all.

Some say because You had to,
I know you came to answer the noble call.

It's all about You,
there is no doubt in my mind.

You came to save souls,
and to bless humanity.

Even when dying on the cross,
You gave one man another change,
to keep his soul from being loss.

It's about You, that's a fact,
to live in an evil world without You,
is to be under constant attack.

It's all about You in everything we do,
You came to save us because You knew,
we could not do it without You.

Thank You God

For Jesus.

For Love.

For Mercy.

For Grace.

For Health.

For Strength.

For our families.

For our jobs.
For our husbands.

For our wives.

For the promise of immortality,
and eternal life.

About the Author

Fannie Minson Hudson is the author of two history books; *"My Cousin, My Kin, My Friend",* published in 2000, and *"History of New Smyrna Black Businesses"* published in 2006.

Hudson's love for books, reading and storytelling began at age three, when her sister Mary introduced her to books.

Hudson writes from the heart, with warmth, truth, past pains, joys and hurts, yet touching and sincere.

Hudson and husband James, resides in New Smyrna Beach, FL.

www.ingramcontent.com/pod-product-compliance
Lightning Source LLC
LaVergne TN
LVHW051204080426
835508LV00021B/2790